CLASSIC ROCK FOR TWO

T0082037

Arrangements by Peter Deneff

ISBN 978-1-5400-6542-1

HAL•LEONARD®

Visit Hal Leonard Online at
www.halleonard.com

Contact Us:
Hal Leonard
7777 West Bluemound Road
Milwaukee, WI 53213
Email: info@halleonard.com

In Europe contact:
Hal Leonard Europe Limited
42 Wigmore Street
Marylebone, London, W1U 2RN
Email: info@halleonardeurope.com

In Australia contact:
Hal Leonard Australia Pty. Ltd.
4 Lentara Court
Cheltenham, Victoria, 3192 Australia
Email: info@halleonard.com.au

BANG A GONG

(Get It On)

ALTO SAXES

Words and Music by
MARC BOLAN

CAN'T FIGHT THIS FEELING

ALTO SAXES

Words and Music by
KEVIN CRONIN

Rock Ballad

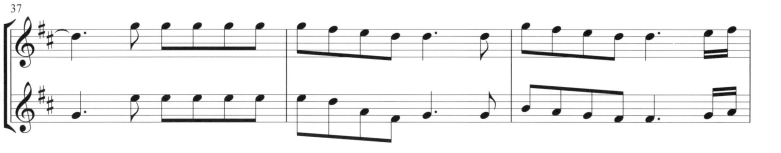

CARRY ON WAYWARD SON

ALTO SAXES

Words and Music by
KERRY LIVGREN

Moderate Rock

COLD AS ICE

ALTO SAXES

Words and Music by MICK JONES
and LOU GRAMM

Medium Rock shuffle

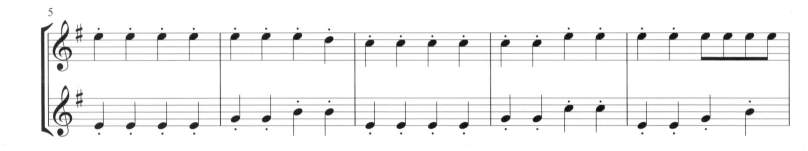

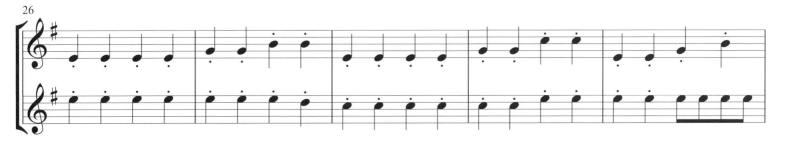

COME ON EILEEN

ALTO SAXES

Words and Music by KEVIN ROWLAND,
JAMES PATTERSON and KEVIN ADAMS

Moderately

COME TOGETHER

ALTO SAXES

Words and Music by JOHN LENNON
and PAUL McCARTNEY

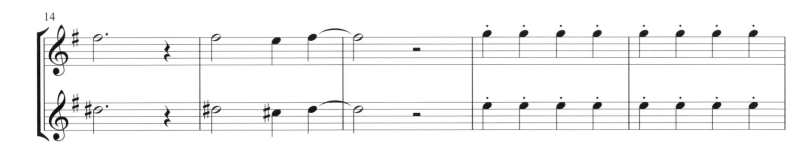

CROCODILE ROCK

ALTO SAXES

Words and Music by ELTON JOHN
and BERNIE TAUPIN

Lively

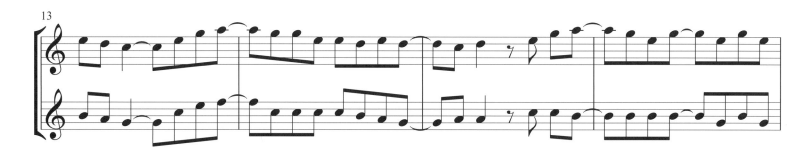

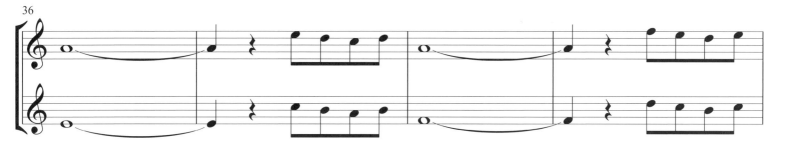

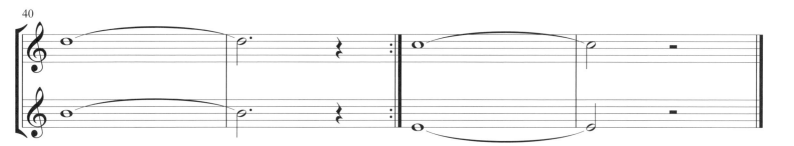

DOWN ON THE CORNER

ALTO SAXES

Words and Music by
JOHN FOGERTY

Moderately

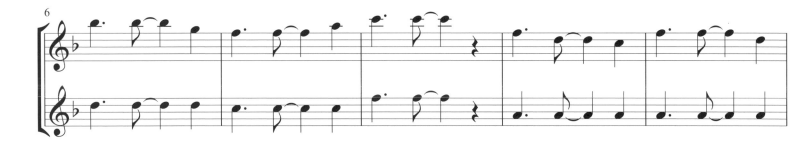

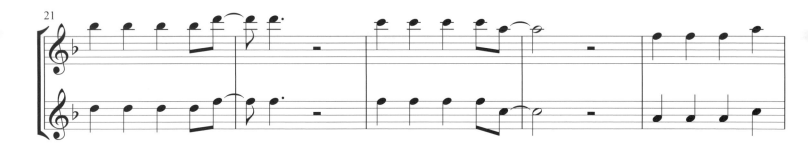

EVERY LITTLE THING SHE DOES IS MAGIC

ALTO SAXES

Words and Music by
STING

Moderately fast

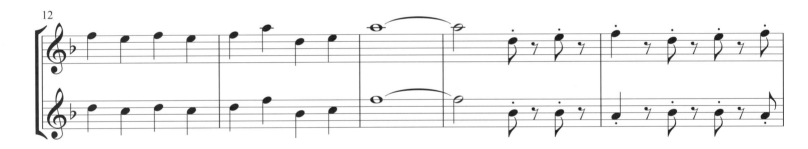

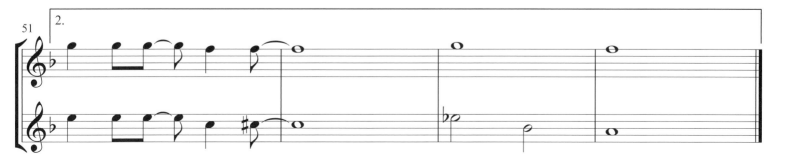

FREE FALLIN'

ALTO SAXES

Words and Music by TOM PETTY
and JEFF LYNNE

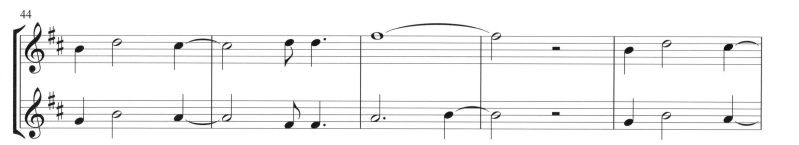

HURTS SO GOOD

ALTO SAXES

Words and Music by JOHN MELLENCAMP
and GEORGE GREEN

Moderate Rock

To Coda

CODA

D.S. al Coda

THE JOKER

ALTO SAXES

Words and Music by STEVE MILLER,
EDDIE CURTIS and AHMET ERTEGUN

Moderately

LIVIN' ON A PRAYER

ALTO SAXES

Words and Music by JON BON JOVI,
DESMOND CHILD and RICHIE SAMBORA

Moderate Rock

To Coda ⊕

1.

2.

D.S. al Coda

CODA ⊕

MAGGIE MAY

ALTO SAXES

Words and Music by ROD STEWART
and MARTIN QUITTENTON

Moderately

MR. ROBOTO

ALTO SAXES

Words and Music by
DENNIS DeYOUNG

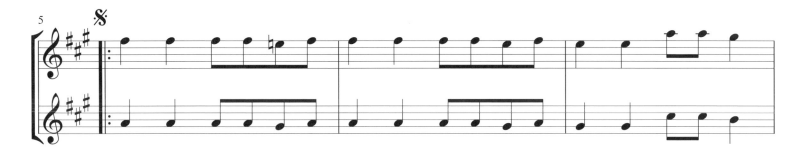

Play 3 times

MONEY FOR NOTHING

ALTO SAXES

Words and Music by MARK KNOPFLER
and STING

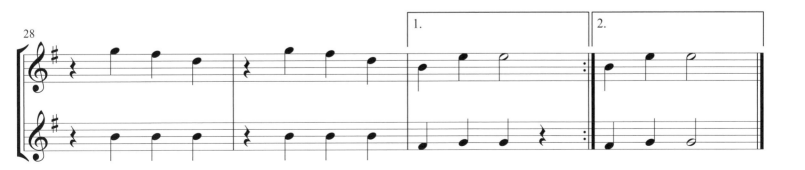

ONE MORE NIGHT

ALTO SAXES

Words and Music by
PHIL COLLINS

Moderate Ballad

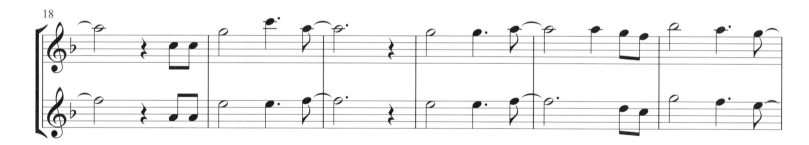

PEACE OF MIND

ALTO SAXES

Words and Music by
TOM SCHOLZ

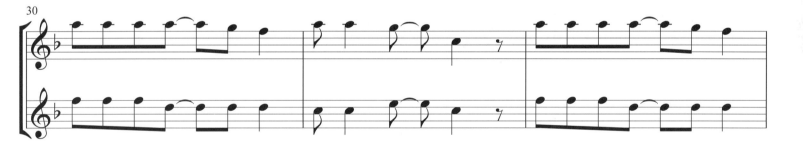

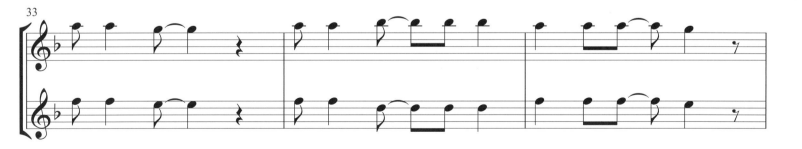

REELING IN THE YEARS

ALTO SAXES

Words and Music by WALTER BECKER
and DONALD FAGEN

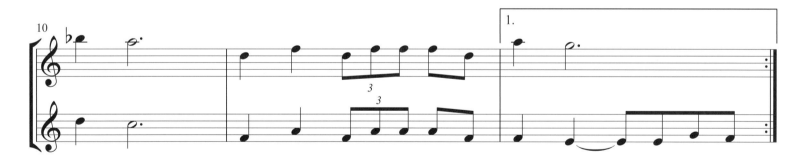

SMOKE ON THE WATER

ALTO SAXES

Words and Music by RITCHIE BLACKMORE,
IAN GILLAN, ROGER GLOVER,
JON LORD and IAN PAICE

Moderate Rock

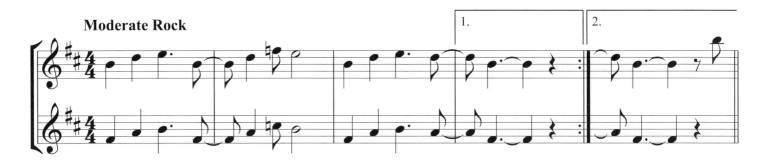

SUMMER OF '69

ALTO SAXES

Words and Music by BRYAN ADAMS
and JIM VALLANCE

Moderate Rock

To Coda

D.C. al Coda

CODA

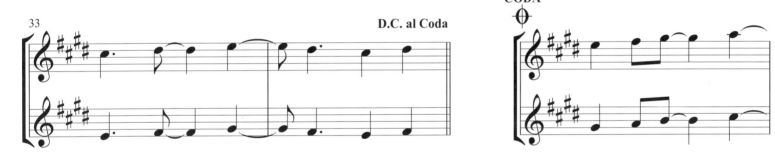

UPTOWN GIRL

ALTO SAXES

Words and Music by
BILLY JOEL

Moderately

YOU'RE THE INSPIRATION

ALTO SAXES

Words and Music by PETER CETERA
and DAVID FOSTER

Rock Ballad

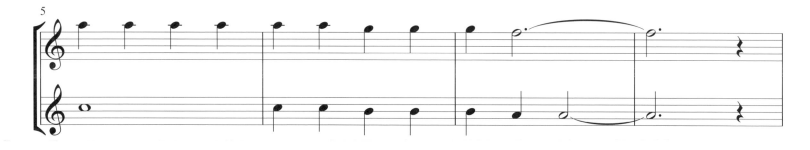

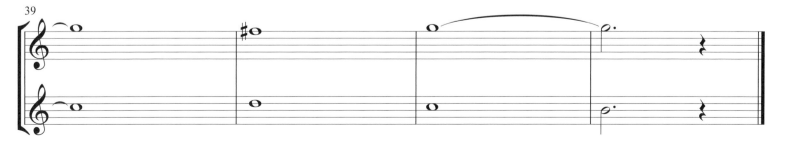